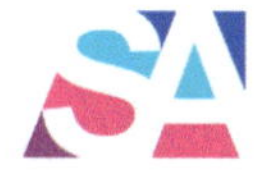

www.WithPhotography.co.uk

SAbstract
28 Claremont Street, Walpole Suite 5,
Surbiton, Surrey, UK, KT6 4RF

86 Days In Lockdown — With Photography
© Sally Hedges Greenwood ARPS

Sally Hedges Greenwood is an Associate of The Royal Photographic Society; a conceptual, contemporary and documentary photographer and author of the With Photography® series of books.

For 76 of these days (from 17 March) Sally ran an online projet for the Facebook group 'SheClicks', which currently has a membership of over 6500 female photographers from all over the globe. Some of Sally's images in this sketchbook were the 'Conversation Starters' that headed up her posts, written to discourage feelings of isolation by encouraging group participation; the posting and sharing of members' own images to comment on.

Sally lives in the county of Dorset in England, United Kingdom.

'Total lockdown officially started in England UK on 23 March 2020 and ended on 31 May. Lockdown in our household started on Saturday 7 March.

Powerless in a way that most had never felt before; I recognised I was in the first stages of trauma: partway between anxiety and paralysis: wanting to escape from that moment but knowing that to do so would put me at risk of impacting the effects of what was happening to me — to us all — as we faced our own mortality in isolation. I turned naturally to photography to help me — to document and create order out of my chaotic mind; to explore and diffuse my emotions.

My photographs are a melange of moments with different layers of meaning. All reveal aspects during that particular period up to 31 May, when England started to relieve some restrictions. Then we started to face the realisation that the virus was here to stay; we had to adjust to a new reality with socio-economic hardships of the like that were as yet unknown to us.'

Sally Hedges Greenwood ARPS
16 July 2020

www.WithPhotography.co.uk
email: Sally@WithPhotography.co.uk

We lived in innocence and ignorance...

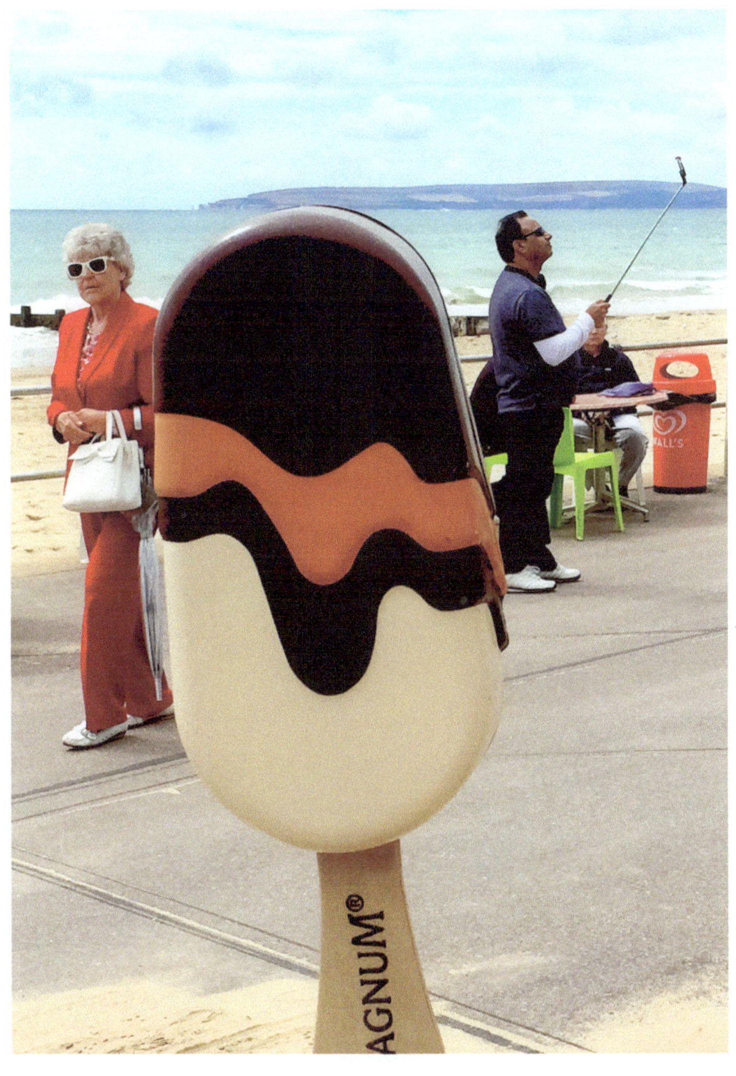

...before

But now, if you are in the wrong place at the wrong time, there is no discrimination...

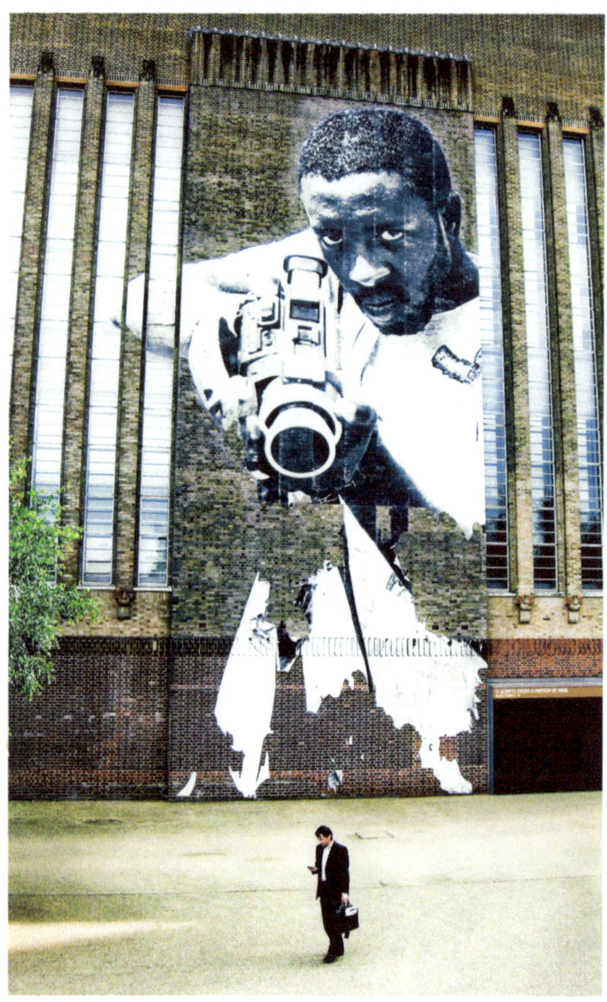

...the virus can strike you down

We are facing our own mortality

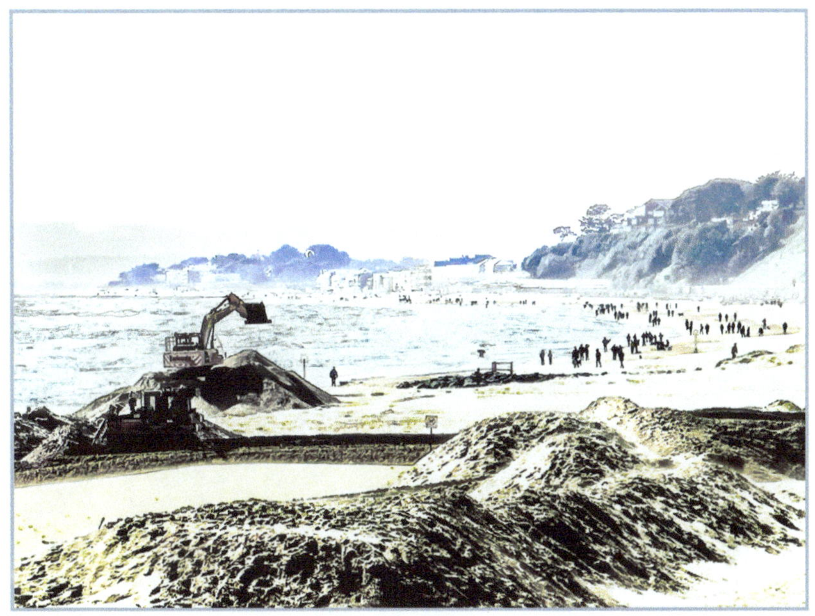

Despite warnings not to, the public flock to open spaces. The beach near us looks surreal —befitting the macabre situation we are now facing — as work continues to clear the devastation created by last month's storms Dennis and Ciara.

21 March

The Prime Minister addresses the nation to
announce extraordinary measures that effectively
put the United Kingdom into 'lockdown'. We are told
to 'Stay home; Protect the NHS; Save Lives'

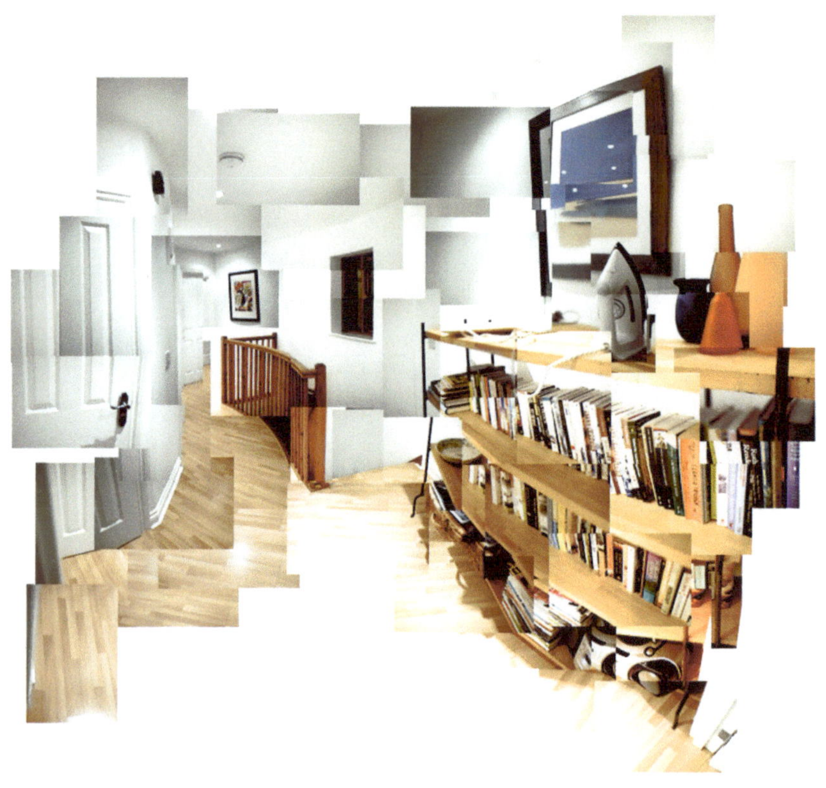

We retreat within four walls...

23 March

...behind closed doors, except for our heroes...

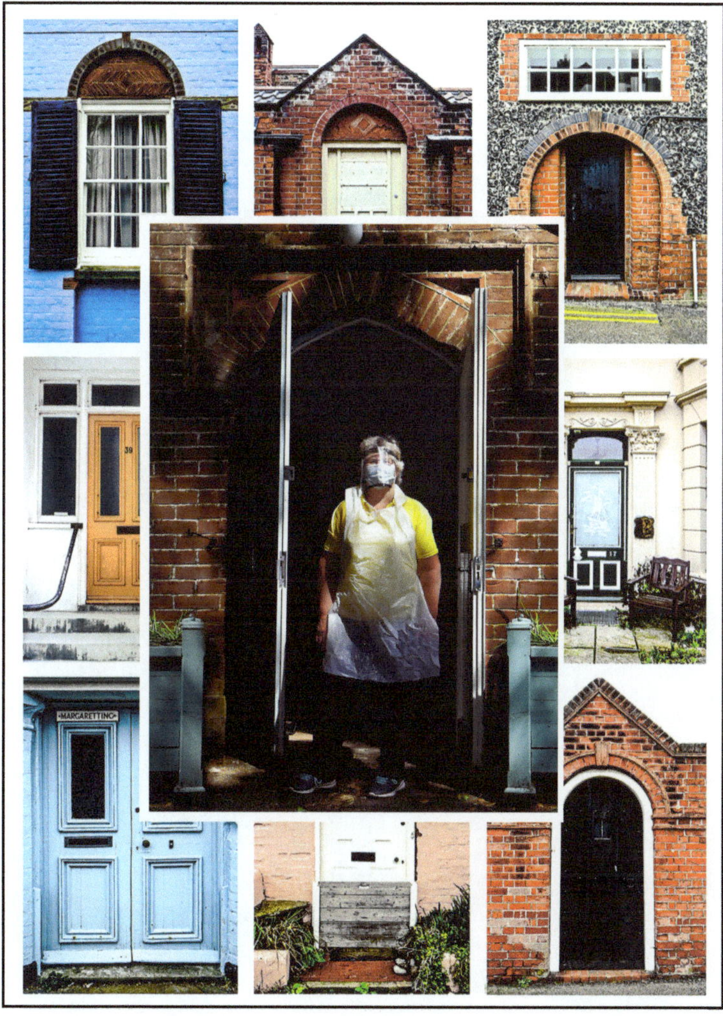

... the front-line workers

...who we applaud from our doorsteps each Thursday at 8pm

Isolation is easier to face together...

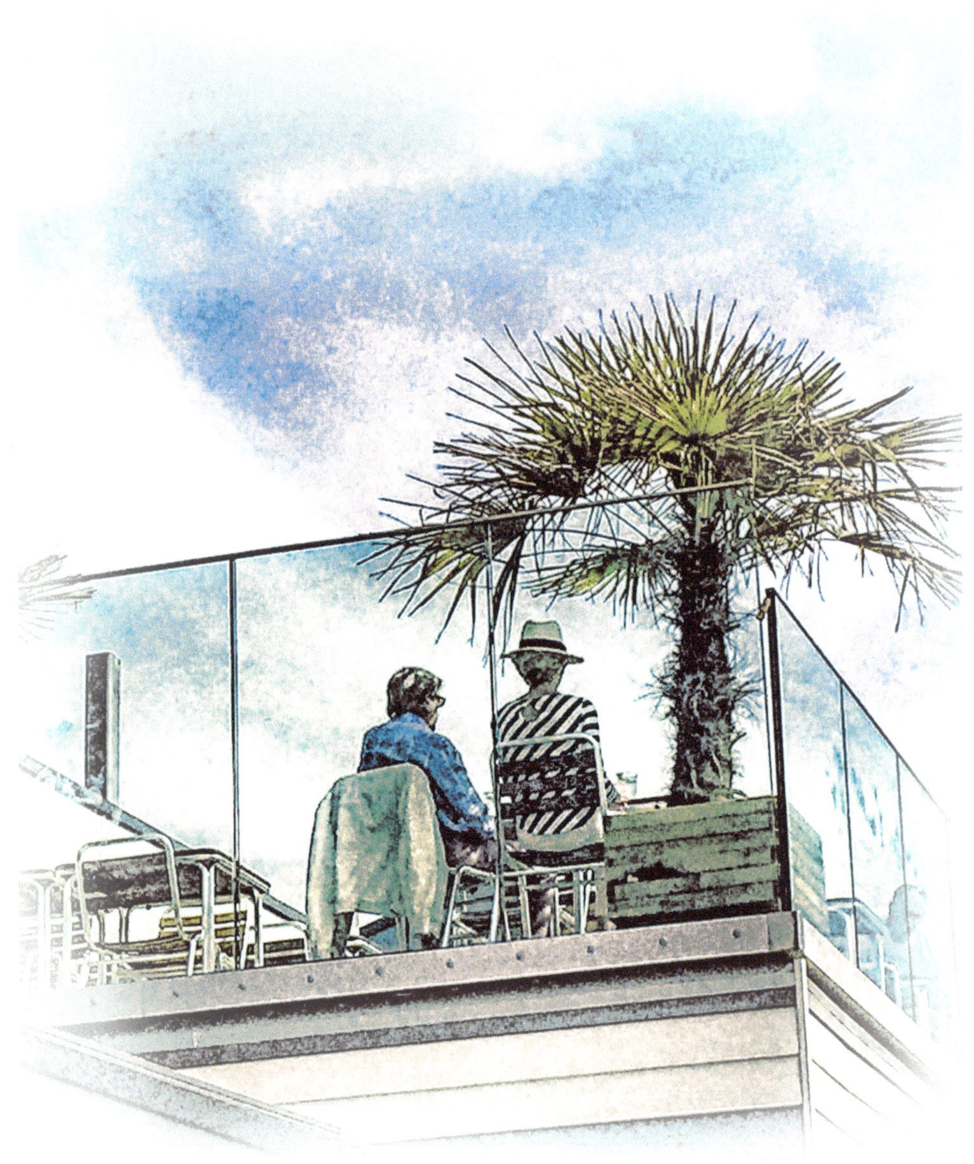

...than if you are alone

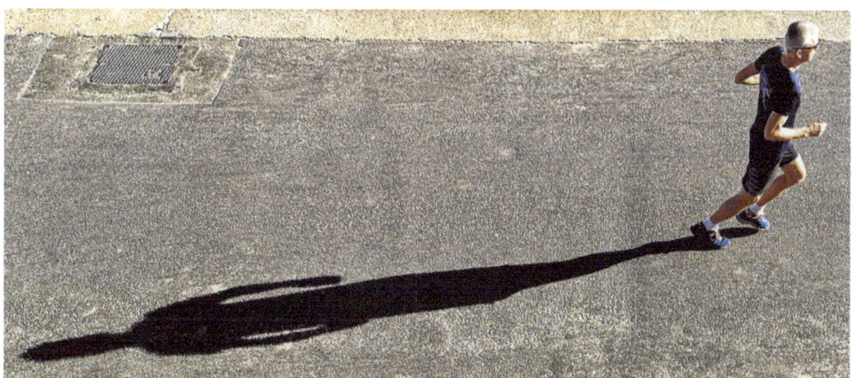

... but not for those who are suffering at the hands of another

The impact of coronavirus in care homes is significant, posing a major threat to vulnerable residents as well as visitors and staff.

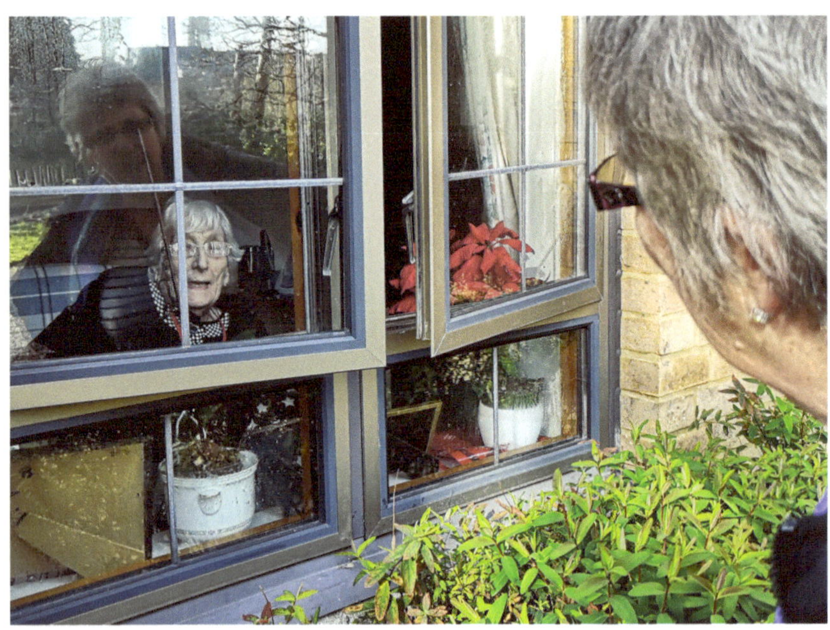

During our allowed exercise time of one hour outside we can walk to see Mum through her window. Shielded in a care home near by, we are also lucky that her room is on the ground floor...

... and just a cycle ride to our daughter, to leave
a surprise on her doorstep on the morning of
her birthday...

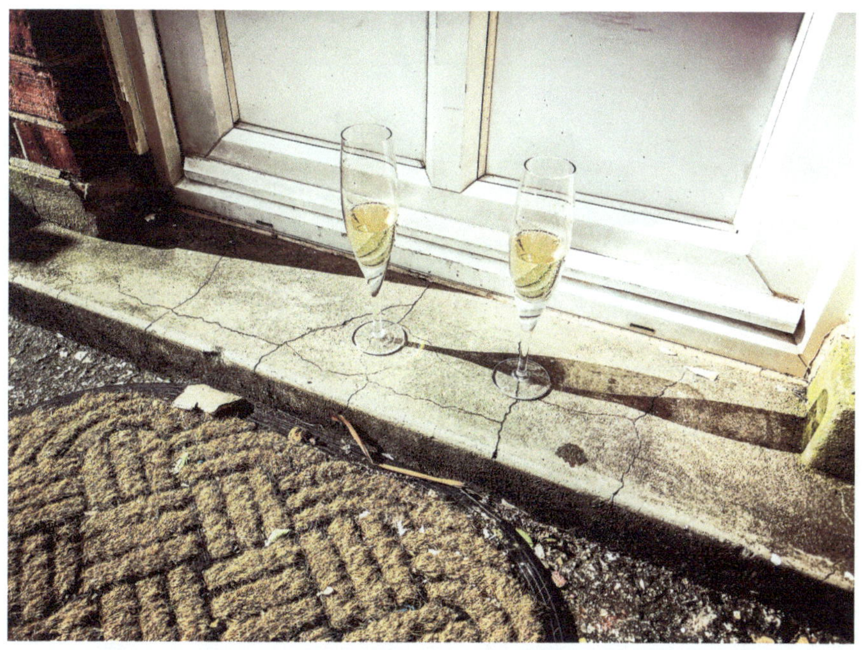

the first lockdown birthday in our family to be
celebrated together 'later',whenever that may be.

Our world is on hold.

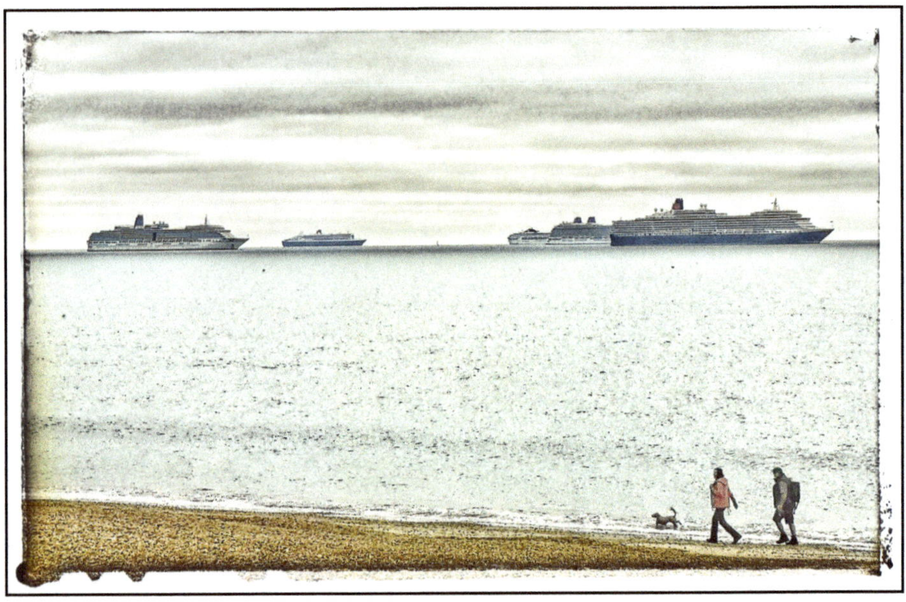

With non-essential travel banned,
tourism is cancelled,..

...events and gatherings are forbidden...

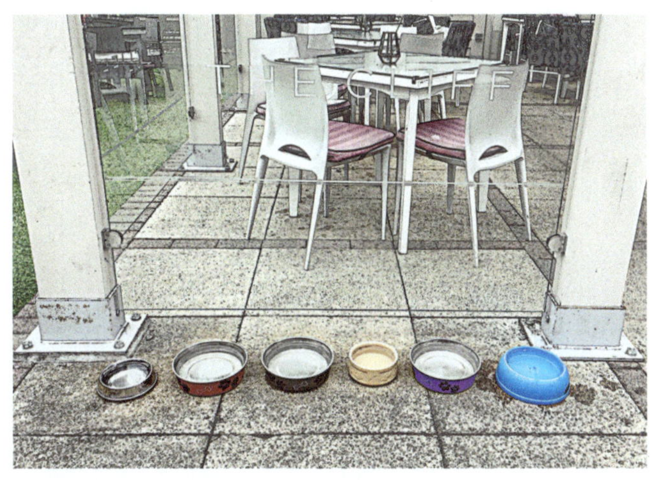

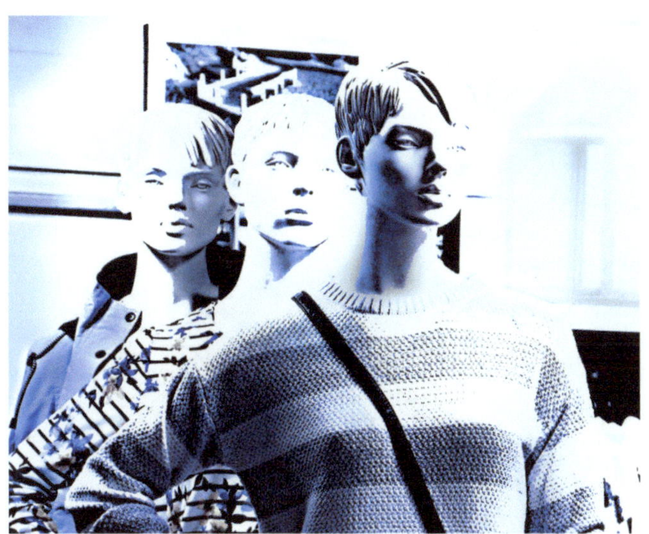

...restaurants and shops are now closed...

With the Performing Arts in crisis...

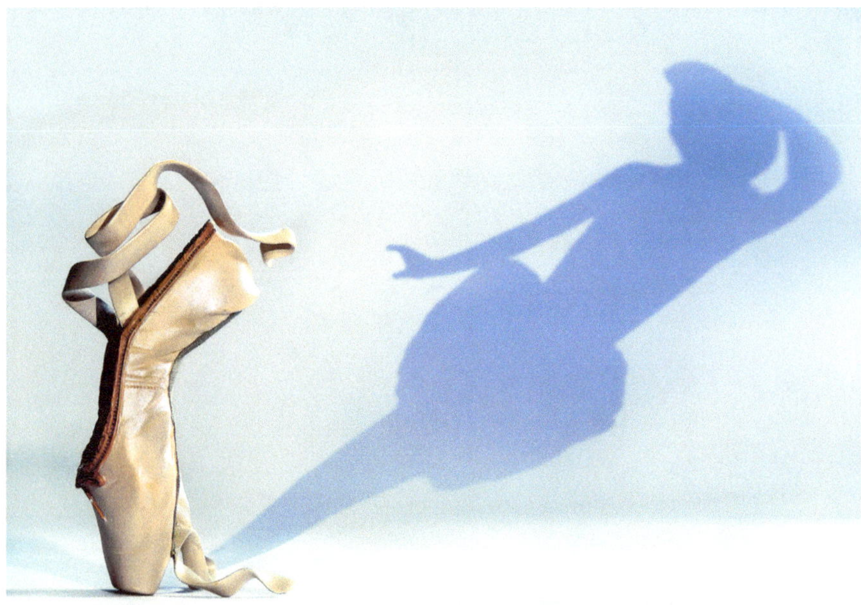

...the best of the best take to the Internet to share performances to a global audience from their homes

Beauty spots and areas of historic interest
are closed....

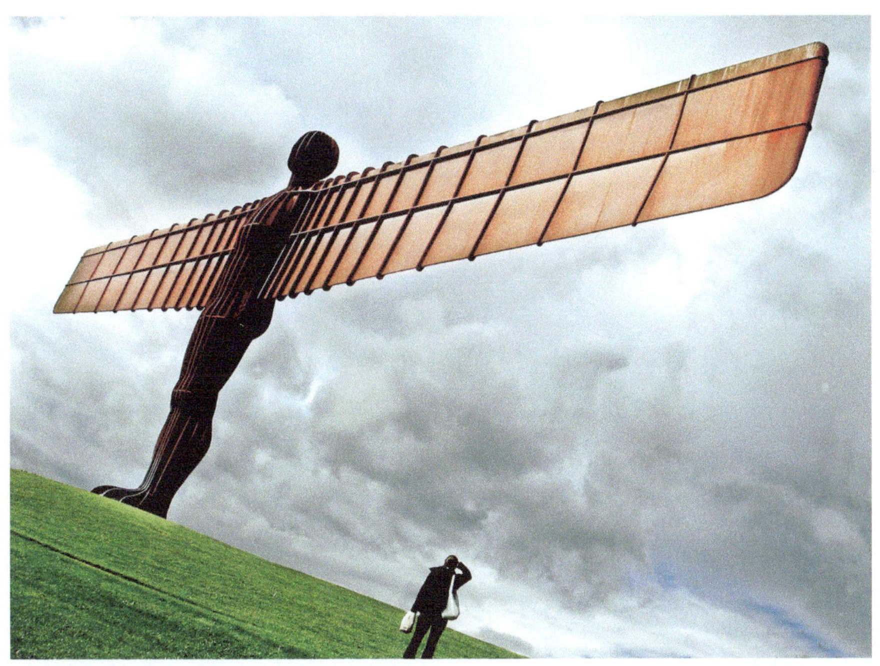

A coronavirus particle is only 125nm
but it is bigger than us all

With churches closed since 17 March, live
services of all denominations are held online.

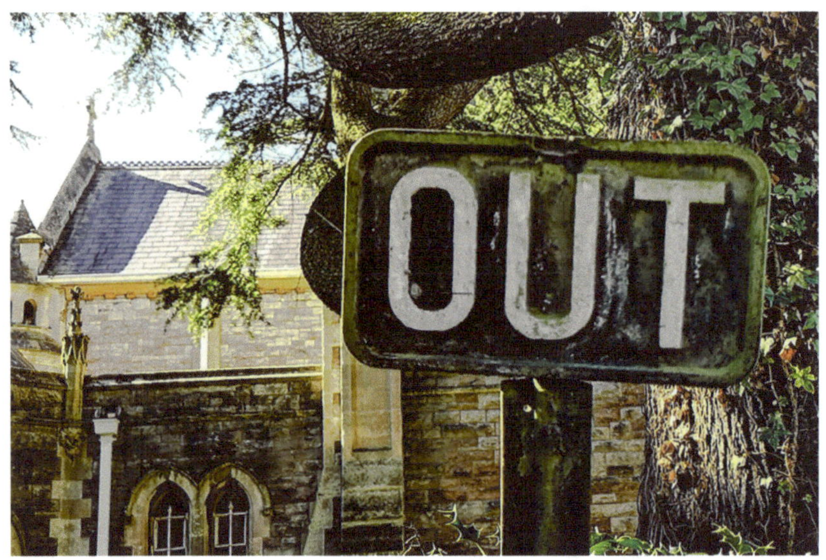

The Pope reads his 'Urbi et Orbi message in St
Peter's basilica with no public in attendance..

Easter Sunday 12 April

We communicate with photography....

at 5am I check my phone,
preferably for no news,...

At midnight my sister, who
I have yet to see this year
had written...'an
awesome moon tonight....

I get up and go to the top
of the garden, to take our
rising sun and reply...
'it's lovely here this
morning too'

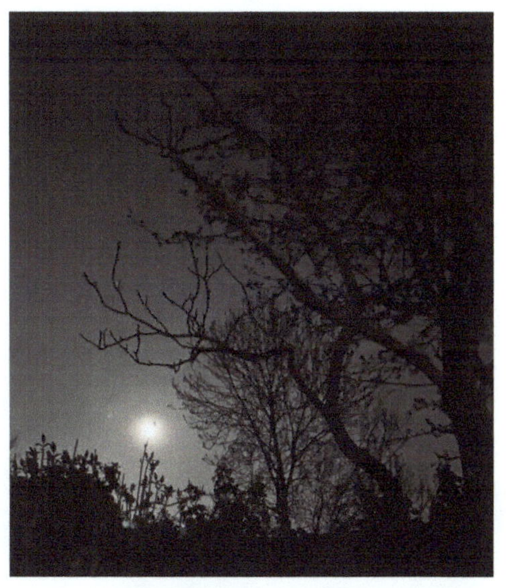

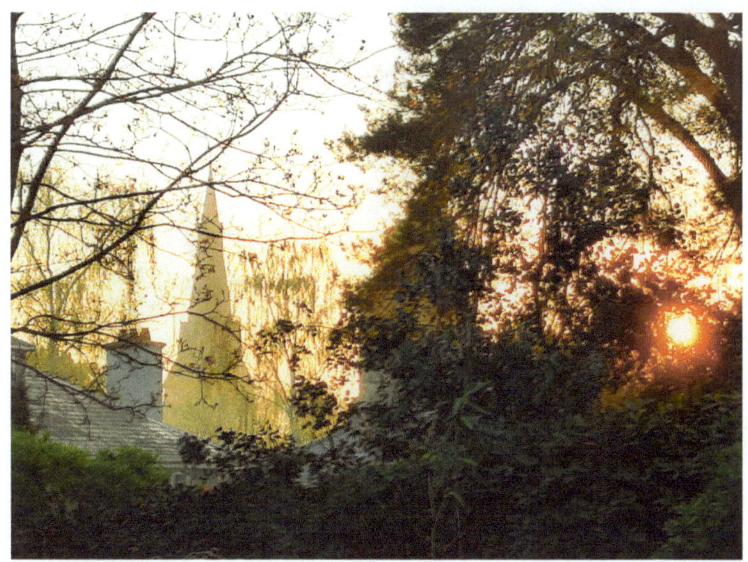

...we try to stay positive; keeping ourselves busy with projects in the home, garden and online...

we zoom; create photographic posts
for the group online; cook nutritious food;
explore the family photo archives;
photograph nature in the garden;
do impossible jigsaws...

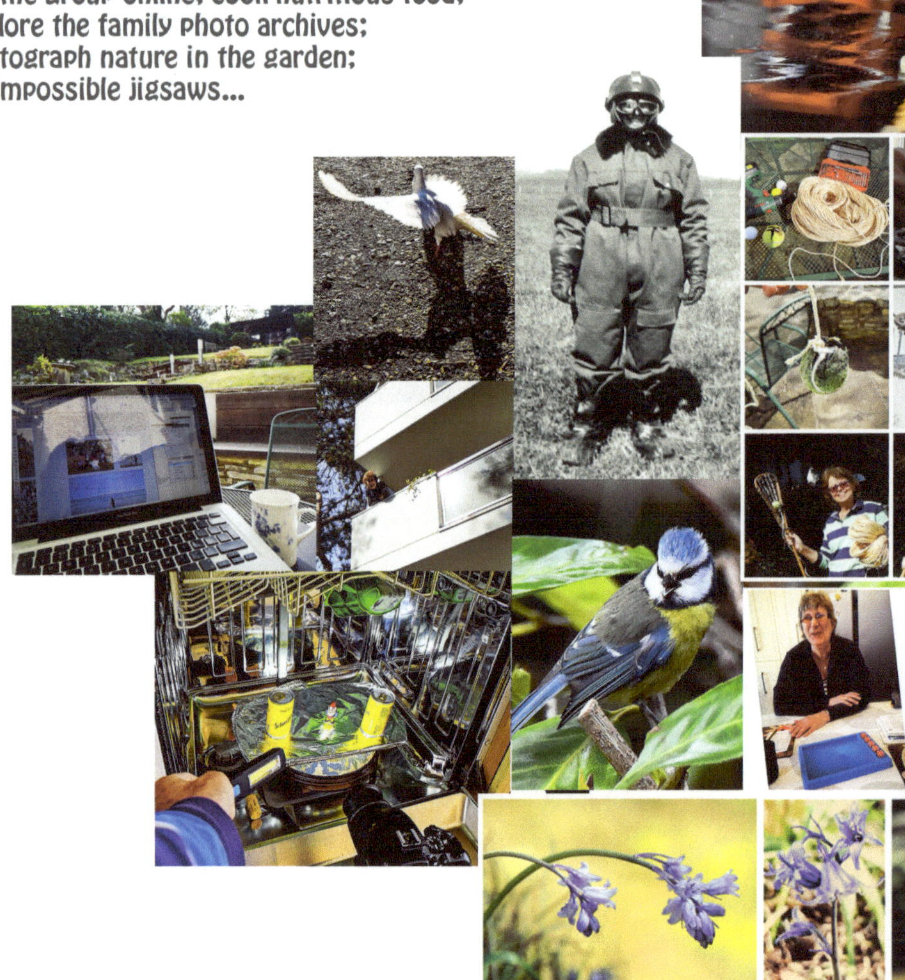

...every day...

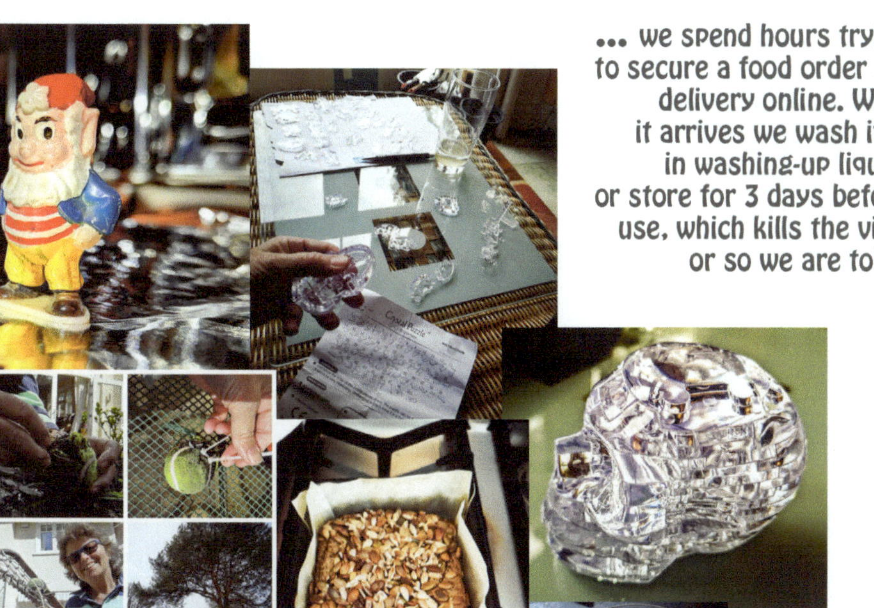

... we spend hours trying
to secure a food order and
delivery online. When
it arrives we wash it all
in washing-up liquid,
or store for 3 days before
use, which kills the virus
or so we are told...

...we abandon adult games like
Bridge in favour of our children's
games (finding them hilariously
funny); we do our one hour
exercise religiously and keep
an eye out for the neighbours
at the same time...

... from 7 March to 31 May

Today we reach the peak... but we don't know that until much later, when many more dark days of death and fear have passed by

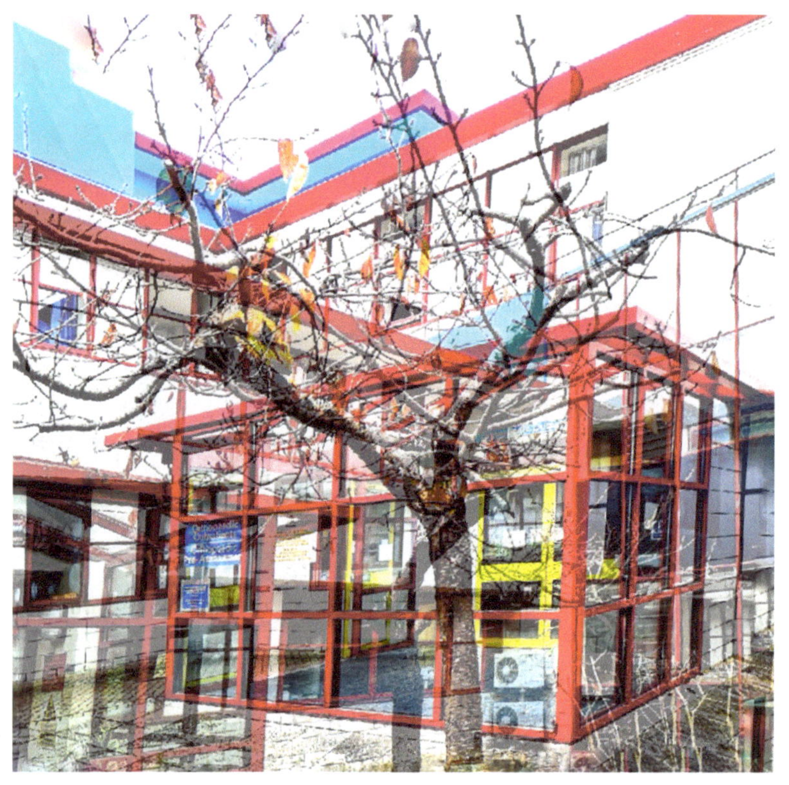

22,300 coronavirus-related deaths in England
and Wales reported up to April 17.

17 April

Keeping things in perspective is hard when there seems that there is no way out

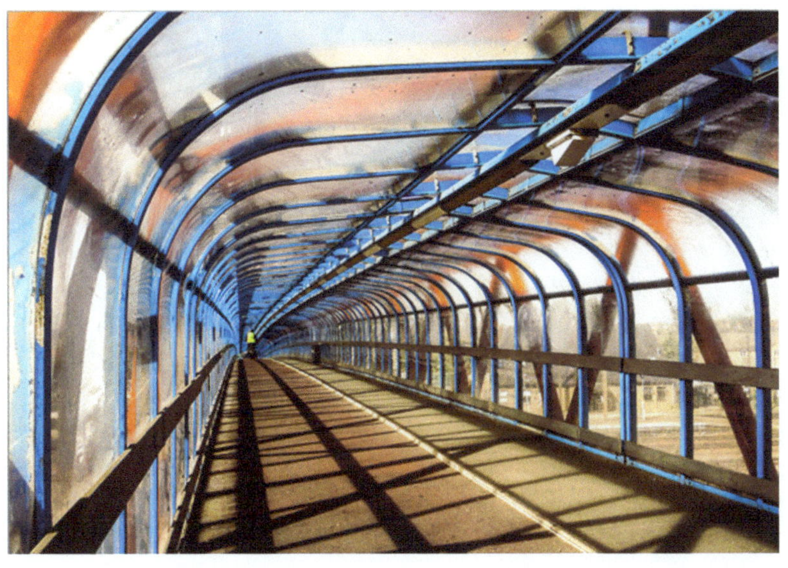

The 75th anniversary of Victory in Europe Day

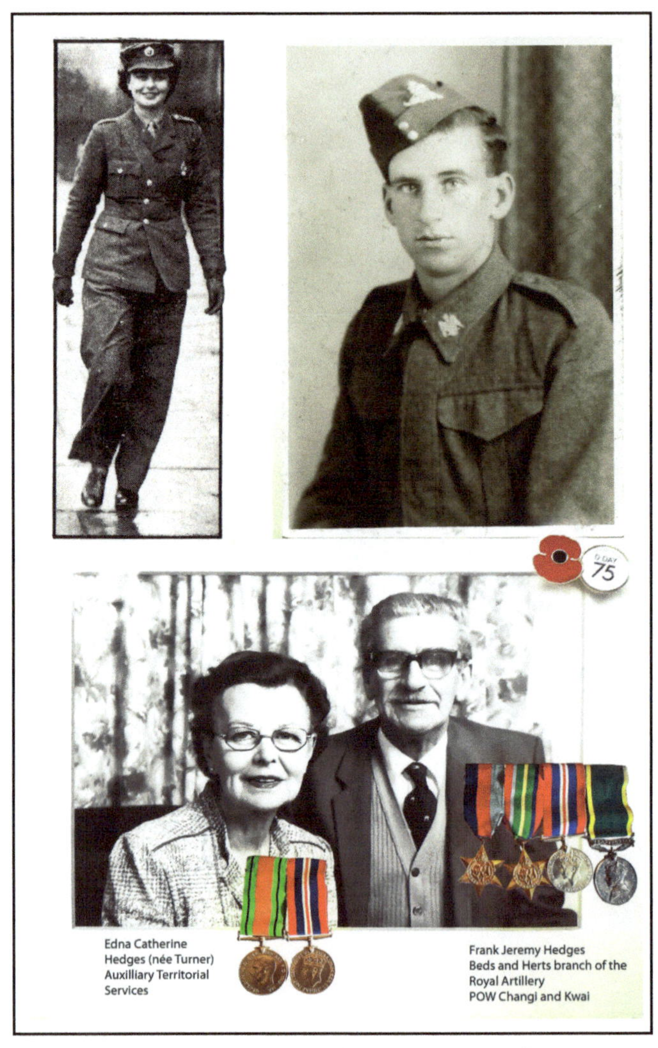

We remember our own...

8 May

...and commemorate in isolation

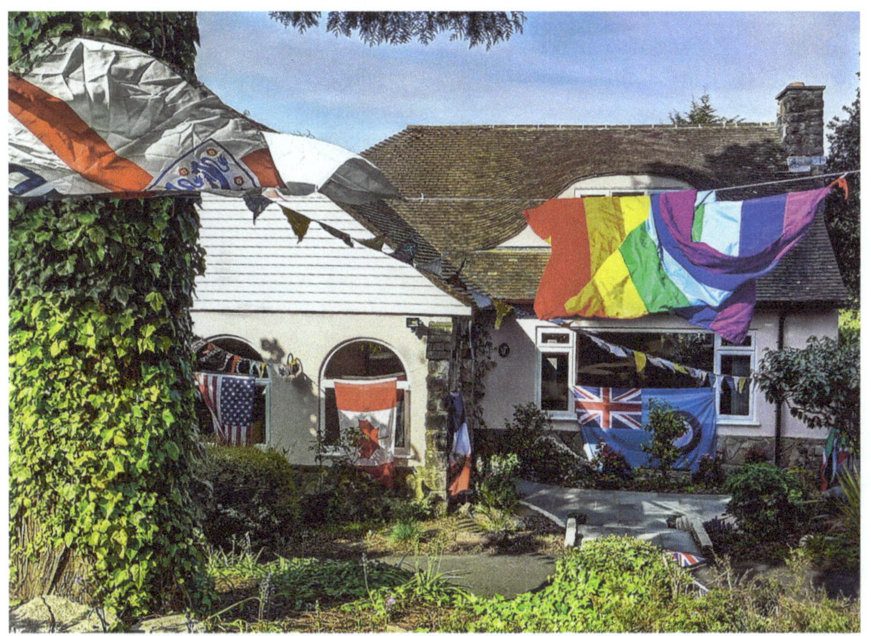

In Westminster yesterday news broke of an
advisor who broke lockdown regulations that
he himself had recommended, causing
general unrest in the country.

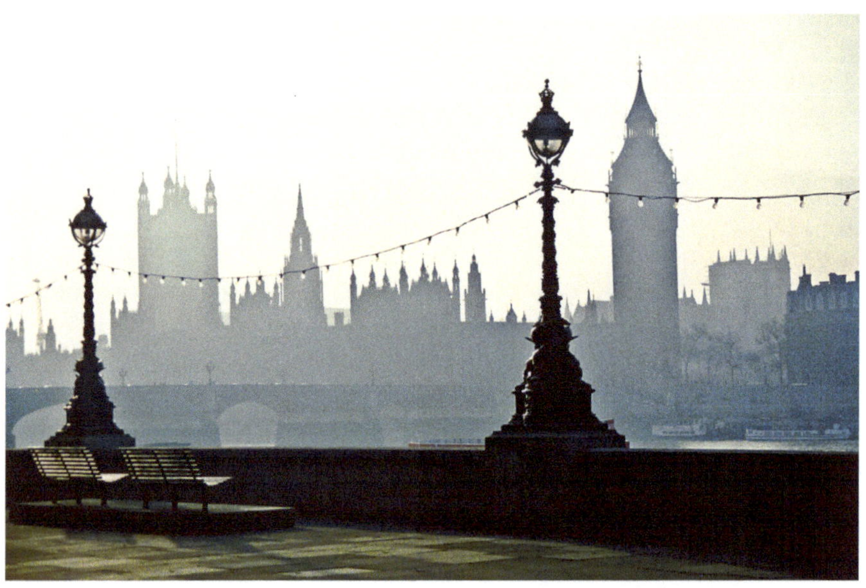

And now today the Transport Minister announces
measures to get more commuters to take up active
travel after the Bank Holiday weekend, which starts
tomorrow...

23 May

Is this a pantomime?

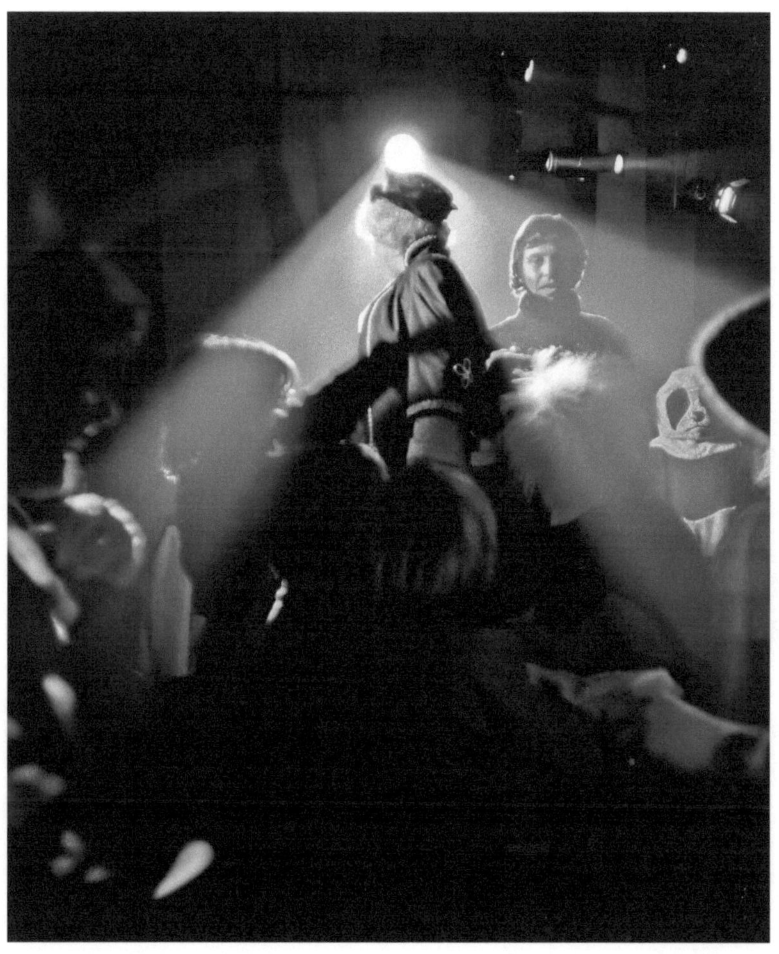

...I wish it was

Suddenly the country seems to be on the move again. We hear the cars back on the roads as our beaches are invaded, with no amenities, not even toilets, open... we're not ready...

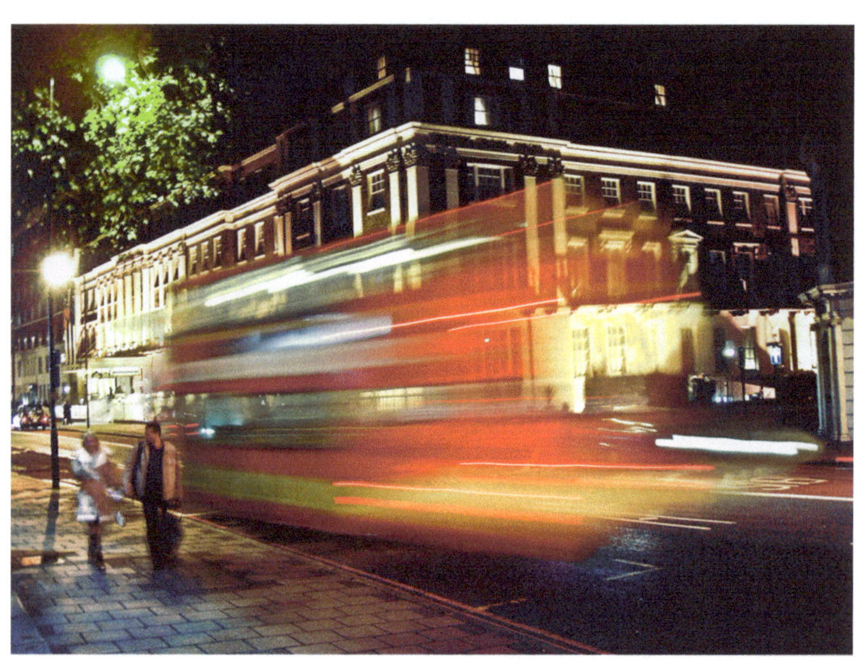

and London commuters brace themselves with fear that a second peak may now commence.

Saturday 24 May

I feel dazed and confused

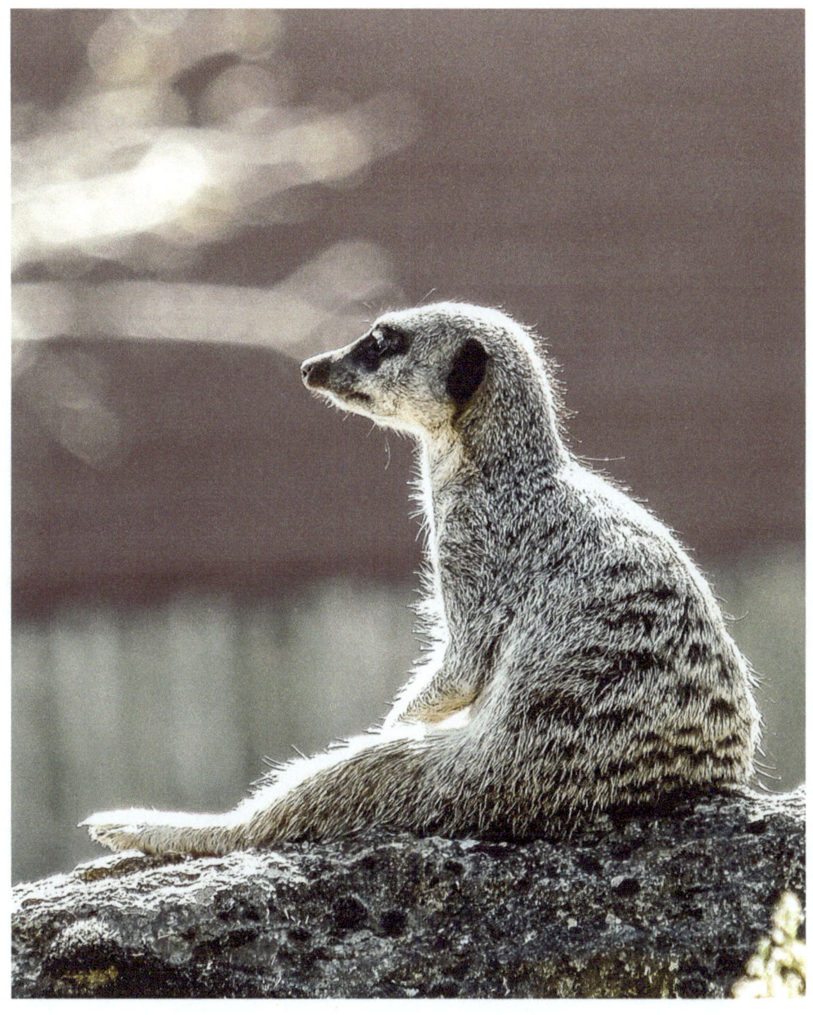

24 May

There is now a divide in the United Kingdom:
The reactionary...

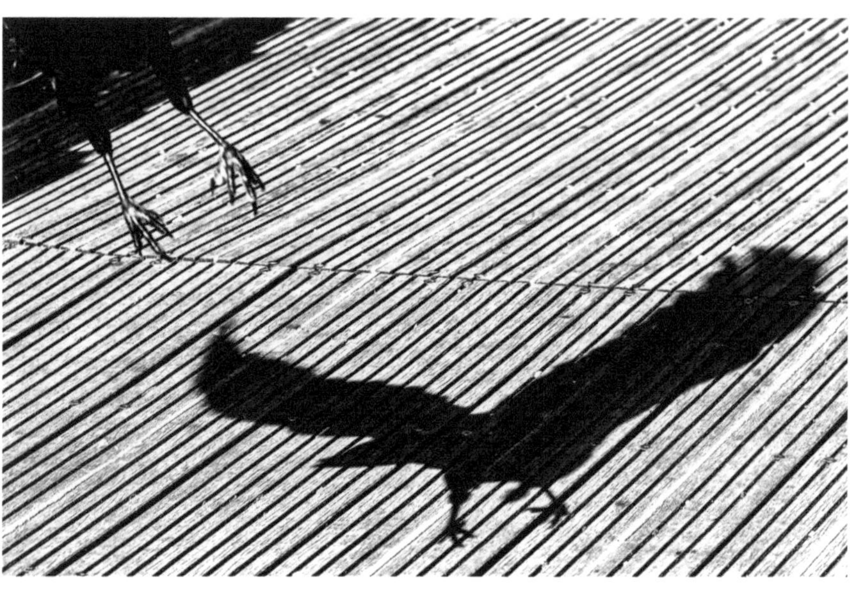

and the more timid and the cautious,
of which I am one.

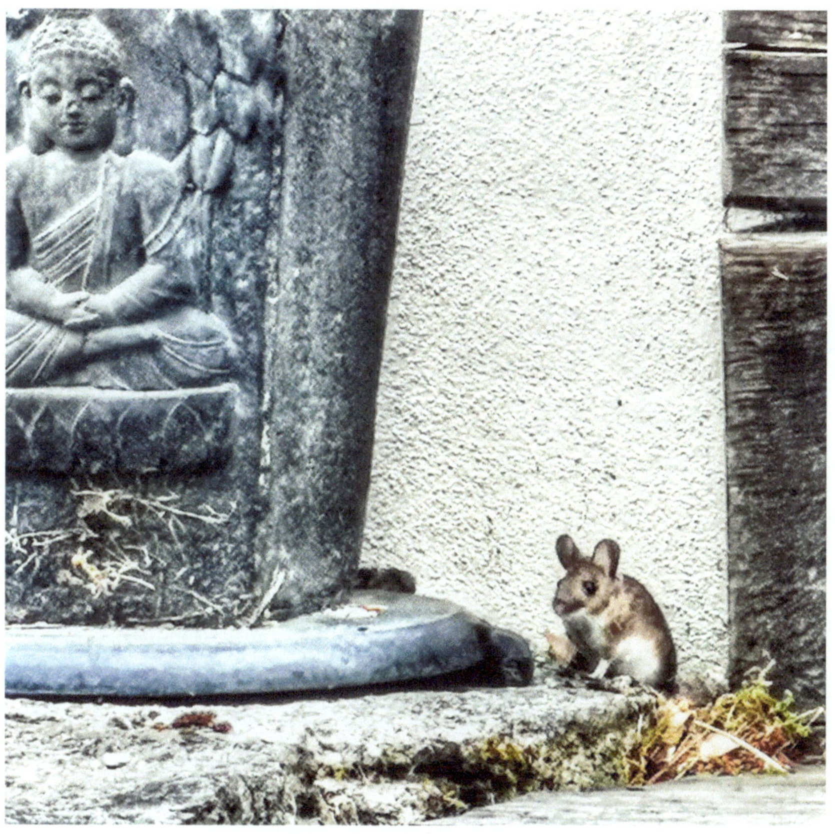

The weather is defiant; the sun shining
from dawn...

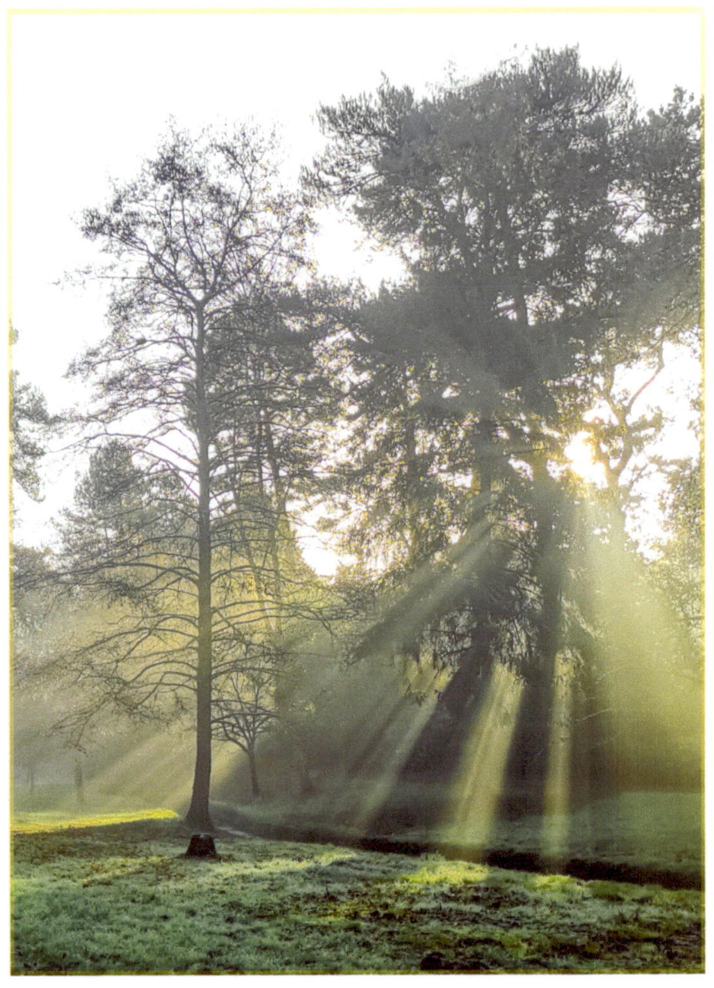

It is surreal. Making isolation more bearable but
harder to accept our new reality

...until dusk

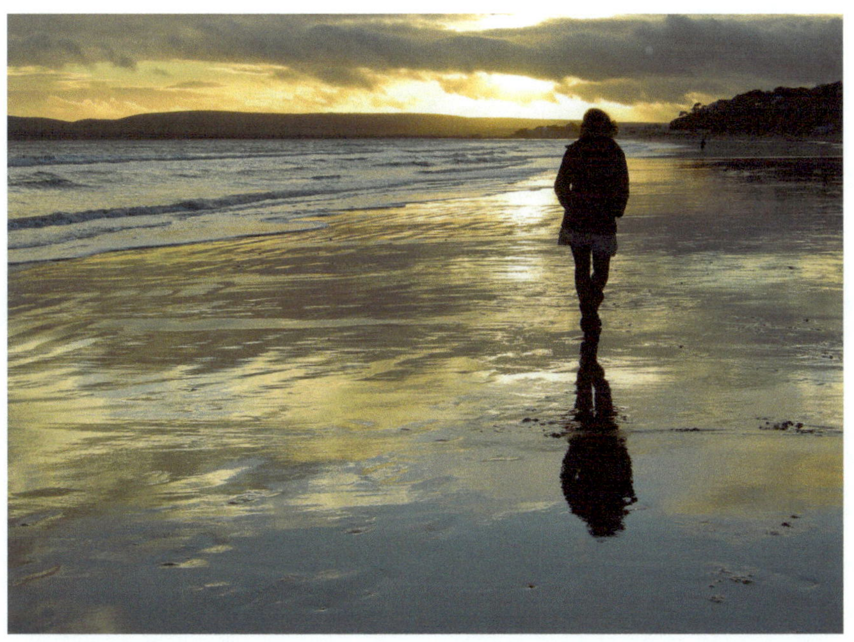

31 May

Written on day 28 of 86 days in Lockdown in the UK

It is April 3rd 2020 (* 3 weeks before the peak of the first wave in the UK of week 17 April)
16,387 deaths were registered in England and Wales, which is the highest weekly total since the second week of January, 2000. 3,475 of those deaths are attributed to COVID-19.

Directives: Hour-long daily press conferences from the government, live from Westminster on the BBC TV at 5pm, with MPs and health officials giving updates on new cases and deaths.

Since 23 March the orders from the government are to "Stay At Home; Protect The NHS; Save Lives" —
the slogan is so successful that there is concern about how the government will convince people when it is safe to go outside again. (Changed to "Stay Alert; Protect The NHS; Save Lives' on May 10th as some restrictions were lifted, which was then criticised for not being a clear enough directive.)

The National Health Service (the NHS): There is a shortage of masks, gowns, gloves for our front-line workers and ventilators for the critically ill. Arenas open up for the overflow of Covid-19 patients including NHS Nightingale at the Excel exhibition centre in London.

Essential service workers are terrified to go to work.   Medical field workers are afraid to go home to their families.

Commerce and Industry: Non-essential stores and businesses are closed by mandate. Self-distancing measures are on the rise. Tape on the floors at grocery stores and others to help keep a distance between shoppers of 2m. Limited number of people inside stores, therefore, queues outside the store doors. Some roads have to be closed to safely accommodate them. Employees are furloughed. Manufacturers, distilleries and other businesses switch their lines to help make visors, masks, hand sanitiser and PPE.

Supplies: Panic buying sets in and we have no toilet paper, no disinfecting supplies, no paper towel, no laundry soap, no hand sanitiser. Shelves are bare. Shopping is only allowed for essentials becoming challenging online with deliveries and click and collect slots booked up for weeks in advance. The supermarkets join forces to help distribution, Tesco takes on 20,000 extra temporary workers 'to feed the nation'.

Education: Going to school is cancelled — GCSE, AS, A level, vocational and technical qualifications will be graded by their teachers and awarded in summer 2020. Universities close; students return to their homes while universities decide for themselves how a student in their final year will be graded.

Sport, leisure, the Arts, nature and religion: parks, trails and entire cities are locked up. Sports seasons are cancelled as are concerts, tours, festivals and entertainment events. Weddings, family celebrations, holiday gatherings too. No masses, churches are closed. Graveyards are shut. The dead are denied wakes or funerals and barely anyone is allowed at the graveside.

Travel: All non-essential travel is banned. Fines are established for breaking the rules. Police are patrolling the streets with barely anyone on the roads. As a result the average price of diesel in the UK, which was £1.16, dropped to £1.11 on 31 March, from £1.28 at the start of the year. Cruise ships companies offer to turn their halted

3 April

fleet into floating hospitals as all holidays are cancelled. Aeroplanes are grounded and stockpiled in airports. People take to cycling and walking. Towns and cities see vast reduction in pollution and nature returns to previously abandoned habitats. We want that to be the part of this situation to continue.

The economy: With the introduction of grants and loans, the (Conservative) government throws money at businesses to try to keep the economy from imploding with grants, loans and a furlough scheme, where the government pays 80% of employees wages rather than have huge numbers made redundant.

(GDP: fell by 19.1% in the 3 months to May 2020, following falls of 10.8% in April and 2.2% in March.)

Socially: Some people are wearing masks and gloves outside. No gatherings of 2 or more (except with people from within a household) are allowed. No socialising with anyone outside of the home. Children's outdoor playgrounds are closed. There is fear for children's mental health, segregated from their peers. All ages take to the Internet using mainly WhatsApp and Zoom to maintain contact: from keeping in touch with loved-ones to the highest level Cabinet meetings.

We are coming to the realisation that long-term changes need to be made with minimal physical contact: hugging and kissing friends, the handshake ... we are heading for a 'new normal'.

We are encouraged to be thankful. Be grateful. Be kind to each other — love one another — support everyone. We are all one!

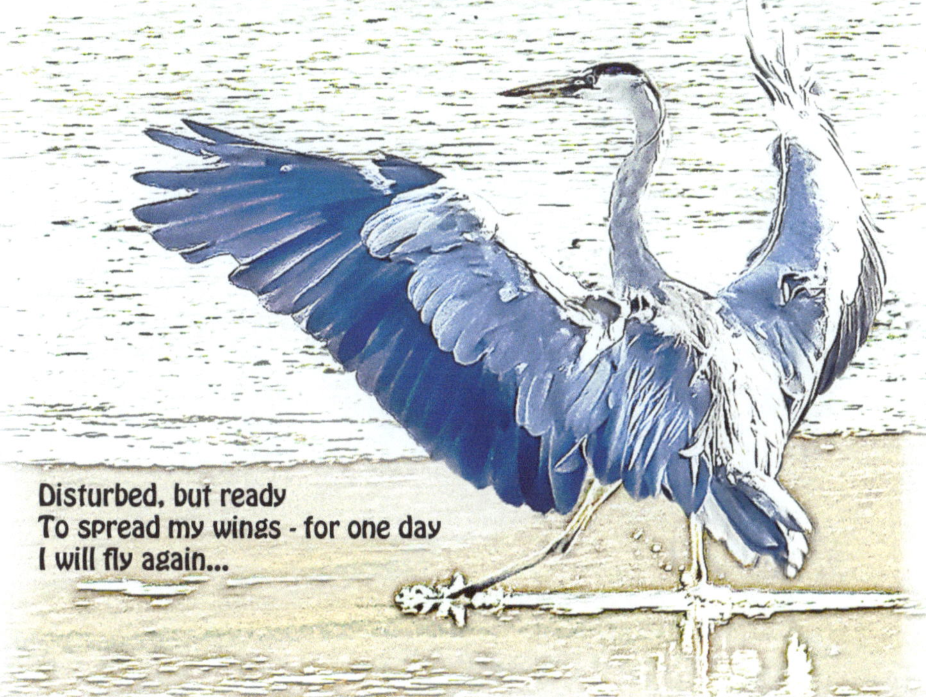

… onwards and then upwards

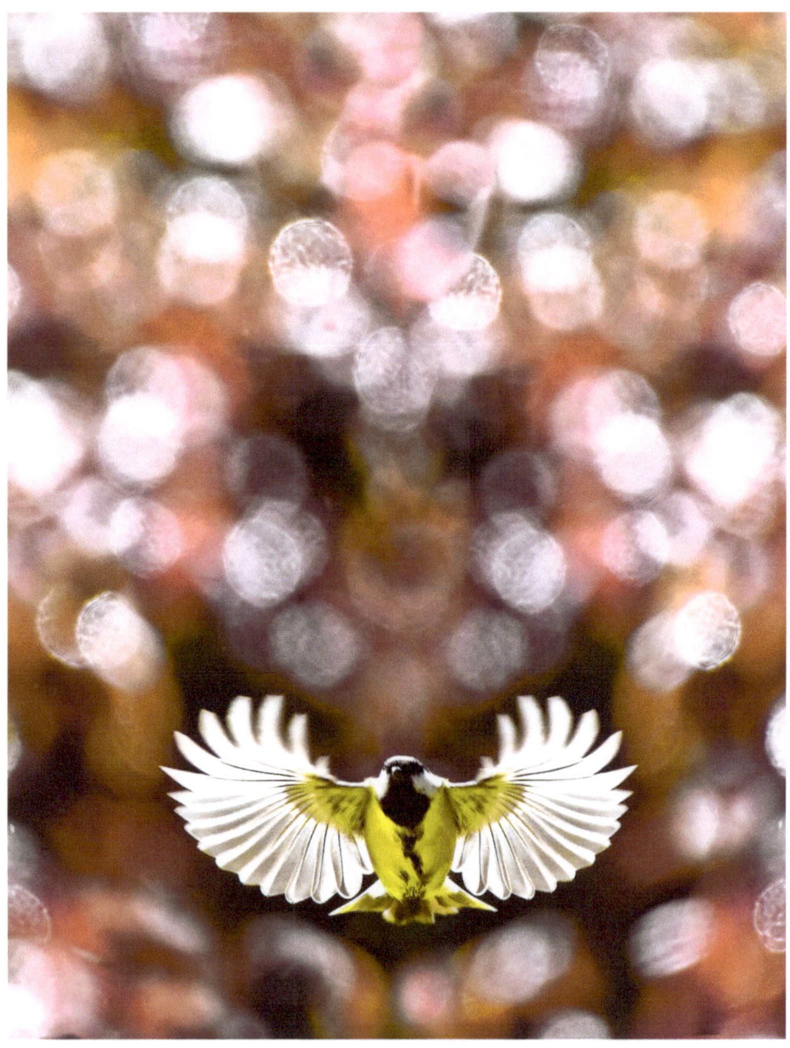

It is 18 July 2020 and the sketchbook project must now finish;
sadly there is no end in sight for my story; we can but wait to see
what happens next. We cannot rewrite what has been written...

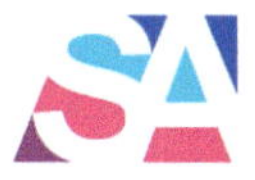

www.WithPhotography.co.uk

SAbstract
28 Claremont Street, Walpole Suite 5,
Surbiton, Surrey, UK, KT6 4RF